How Things Are Made

Sand to Glass

By Inez Snyder

Children's Press®
A Division of Scholastic Inc.
New York / Toronto / London / Auckland / Sydney
Mexico City / New Delhi / Hong Kong
Danbury, Connecticut

Photo Credits: Cover © Mark A. Johnson/Corbis; p. 5 © Bruce Burkhardt/Corbis.; p. 7 © David Lees/Corbis; p. 9 © H. David Seawell/Corbis; pp. 11, 13 Courtesy of Owens-Illinois, Inc.; p. 15 © Juan Silva/Getty Images; p. 17 © Wolfgang Kaehler/Corbis; p. 19 © Attal Serge/Corbis Sygma; p. 21 © Tom Stewart/Corbis

Contributing Editor: Shira Laskin
Book Design: Mindy Liu

Library of Congress Cataloging-in-Publication Data

Snyder, Inez.
    Sand to glass / by Inez Snyder.
    p. cm. — (How things are made)
    Includes index.
    ISBN 0-516-25199-6 (lib. bdg.) — ISBN 0-516-25529-0 (pbk.)
    1. Glass—Juvenile literature. 2. Glass manufacture—Juvenile literature.
    3. Sand—Juvenile literature. I. Title. II. Series: Snyder, Inez.
    How things are made.

    TP857.3.S65 2005
    666'.1—dc22

                                                    2005003817

Contents

Glass is made from sand.

5

First, sand is mixed with other **ingredients**.

7

Next, the sand is **melted** in a hot oven.

The oven turns the sand into **liquid** glass.

9

A **machine** shapes the liquid glass into **bottles**.

As the glass bottles cool, they become hard.

They also change color.

cooling
glass

13

After the glass bottles have cooled, people look at them **carefully**.

They make sure the bottles are not broken.

14

Next, the glass bottles are sent to **factories**.

The bottles can be filled with different things.

These glass bottles are filled with milk.

People can drink milk from a glass.

Glass can be used in many ways.

New Words

bottles (**bot**-uhlz) glass containers with narrow necks and no handles

carefully (**kair**-fuhl-ee) done well with a lot of thought

factories (**fak**-tuh-reez) buildings where people and machines make a large number of things

ingredients (in-**gree**-dee-uhnts) the items that something is made of

liquid (**lik**-wuhd) wet or able to be poured

machine (muh-**sheen**) something that is made to do work or to help make other things

melted (**mel**-ted) turned from a solid into a liquid after being heated

To Find Out More

Books
From Sand to Glass
by Shannon Zemlicka
Lerner Publications

Glass
by Claire Llewellyn
Scholastic Library Publishing

Web Site
Kids Net Junior: Glass Stories
http://www.glassworks.org/kidsnet/kto5/default.html
Learn about the history of glass, how glass is made, and
how glass is recycled on this Web site.

Index

About the Author
Inez Snyder writes books to help children learn how to read.

Reading Consultants
Kris Flynn, Coordinator, Small School District Literacy, The San Diego County Office of Education

Shelly Forys, Certified Reading Recovery Specialist, W.J. Zahnow Elementary School, Waterloo, IL

Paulette Mansell, Certified Reading Recovery Specialist, and Early Literacy Consultant, TX